Summary

of

Jon Gordon's

The Energy Bus

10 Rules to Fuel Your Life, Work, and Team with Positive Energy

by
Swift Reads

Table of Contents

Overview

The Energy Bus: 10 Rules to Fuel Your Life, Work, and Team with Positive Energy (2007) by Jon Gordon is an allegorical tale that teaches readers to cultivate an optimistic attitude for increased personal and professional fulfillment. The book focuses on the fictional story of a miserable worker named George whose pessimism has nearly cost him both his job and his marriage. When George is forced to take the bus to work for two weeks, he meets a charismatic driver, Joy, who teaches him 10 rules for better living. Each rule offers readers a way to take control of their emotional energy, and thus attract individuals who can help them meet their goals.

One Monday morning, George discovers his car has a flat tire. His spare is flat too; his wife told him to fix the spare, but he didn't make time, and now he's without a ride to the office on the morning of an important meeting. His team is launching a new light bulb soon, and if the launch isn't a success then George will be out of a job. When he asks his wife for a ride, she tells him she can't take him, and chides him for thinking that his schedule is the only important one. Left with no other options, George reluctantly takes his wife's advice and walks to the nearest bus stop.

When the bus pulls up, the driver greets him cheerfully, noting that she hasn't seen him before. She introduces herself as Joy, and tells George that he boarded her bus for a reason. George acts surly in the face of Joy's optimism, but Joy persists, pointedly telling him that he can either choose to learn from the challenges he faces, or he can simply complain about his misfortune and face more misery in the future. George gets off the bus as quickly as possible, hoping to never see the driver again. Later that day, however, he learns that a flat tire was not the only thing wrong with his car; his brakes are faulty, and need to be replaced. The repairs will take two weeks. In the meantime, George will have to take the bus.

George decides to walk home, and uses the extra time to think about his miserable situation. His wife has threatened to leave him because of his sour attitude, and his job is in jeopardy. When he was younger, George was praised for his abilities and ambition, but now everything in his life seems to be going wrong. That night and the next day, George resolves to change, though he's unsure where to start.

Joy doesn't drive the bus on Tuesday. On Wednesday, however, she greets George again with her wide smile. Joy reminds him that he is there for a reason, which she explains is to learn her 10 rules for leading a happier, more prosperous life. George resists at first, but eventually agrees. Before Joy stops at George's office building, she teaches him the first rule: every person is responsible for the direction his or her life has taken. Although bosses, spouses, and other important figures in a person's life can provide advice and expertise, they should not be given control over the actual decisions a person makes. Joy gives George a small piece of homework to complete before they next see each other. It is a sheet of paper that asks him to decide what kind of future he wants for his life, his career, and his relationships.

George is still skeptical of how much Joy's rules will help him improve his life and career, but he decides to give her advice a try. Over the next two weeks, George continues to learn from Joy, and gradually becomes more positive and energetic. He uses the 10 rules to unify and energize his team. Together, he and the team successfully launch the new light bulb, which saves his career. His wife even tells him that he is acting like his old self again. By practicing positivity and taking responsibility for his actions, George fixes the overwhelming problems in his life and finds happiness. Even after his car is repaired, George decides to continue taking Joy's bus because she has helped him put his life back on track.

Key Insights

1. Focusing on a goal every day can help people achieve their ambitions.

2. Developing a positive attitude can provide the energy necessary to achieve a given goal.

3. To succeed, leaders must invite others to partner with them in their efforts.

4. Leaders do not allow negative attitudes or team members to derail their efforts.

5. Positive attitudes attract new talented workers and motivate existing employees to do their best.

6. To retain their trust and loyalty, leaders must show genuine love and concern for their employees.

7. Employees and leaders alike must find greater meaning for their work if they wish to stay productive.

8. Leaders must remember to enjoy life, instead of just treating each day as an opportunity to gain money and accolades.

Key Insight 1

Focusing on a goal every day can help people achieve their ambitions.

Analysis

One day on the bus, Joy reveals the second law to George: that envisioning positive results allows people to move closer to achieving their goals. Everything in the universe is made up of energy, including thoughts. Pessimistic thoughts tend to attract negative outcomes, but optimistic thoughts bring about positive change. When people think about their desires, they increase their ability to bring those desires into reality.

Mentally focusing on goals is so effective that athletes will enhance their performance by picturing themselves playing at an optimum level. Some entrepreneurs employ this method as well, especially when developing strategies for improving their businesses or launching new products. In *Rise and Grind: Outperform, Outwork, and Outhustle Your Way to a More Successful and Rewarding Life* (2018), author Daymond John interviews Michael Parrella, an entrepreneur who started the popular gym chain iLoveKickboxing. Although most business executives get up early and immediately start tackling their to-do lists, Parrella starts his mornings off on a quieter note. He spends the first 30 minutes to an hour of his day lying down in bed, thinking about what he needs to accomplish to strengthen his company. The tranquil space allows Parrella to gather his thoughts and focus his energy, so that he can remain on task for the rest of the day. At the end of his work day, he tries to set aside his business altogether so he can focus on his wife and children. Building in specific time periods for quiet contemplation and for spending time with family gives Parrella the chance to recharge, which allows him to keep his goals in perspective and avoid burnout.

Key Insight 2

Developing a positive attitude can provide the energy necessary to achieve a given goal.

Analysis

Everyone faces challenges in life. However, everyone has a choice in how to deal with stressful situations. For example, if a woman is struggling to meet her company's quota, she can either see it as an insurmountable problem or as an opportunity to improve her skills. Being positive will give her more energy to tackle her tasks, whereas being negative about obstacles will drain her of motivation. Joy's third rule requires adherents to look at problems with a positive attitude, and to use that positivity to increase their vitality.

A 2017 *New York Times* column explains that a chronically negative person might find it easier to change his or her larger perspective by attempting first to find joy in small, everyday moments. University of North Carolina psychologist Barbara Fredrickson explains that the brain is capable of creating new pathways throughout a person's life, so even if people have struggled with being positive in the past, they can teach themselves how to look at life more optimistically. Fredrickson recommends that anyone who wants to become more positive try cultivating pro-social behaviors, like being generous toward others and taking time to develop better relationships with loved ones. Practicing intellectual activities and hobbies, such as learning a new language, can also lead to more positivity. The key is to make sure that any new activity or strategy is approached in small stages. For example, if a negative person tries to learn piano, but thinks he will master the instrument in two weeks, then he sets himself up for future negativity because he has set an unobtainable standard for himself.

Key Insight 3

To succeed, leaders must invite others to partner with them in their efforts.

Analysis

A week before the launch of the new light bulb, Joy introduces George to the fourth rule: successful leaders ask for their employees' help. To impress his bosses, George needs to convince members of his team that his leadership is sound and his strategies are worth following. George meets with his team members and asks them to back his efforts. Most say yes, but a few decline, saying that they are afraid George will fail and jeopardize their own jobs. Those employees who decline help George learn the fifth rule — he cannot worry about those who are not willing to help him. Instead, he must focus on achieving his ambitions with the help of the rest of his team.

When businesses look for workers who can help them accomplish their goals, it's important to first develop criteria for the types of candidates they need. In a 2015 *Inc.* article, Aaron Skonnard, chief executive officer of the professional development site Pluralsight, explains how his company searches for new hires when trying to fill open positions. Instead of searching for the best professionals in a given field, Skonnard looks for workers who strive to improve their skills a tiny bit each day, and who are committed to working as a team. People who have numerous accolades attached to their names often have oversized egos, and may focus more on netting individual accomplishments than helping their team solve problems. Skonnard said he additionally looks for traits that his best employees share, such as a tendency to be kind or a penchant for optimism. If a candidate shows those personal qualities during an interview, he or she likely will have a temperament that complements those who are already working at the business. By developing an idea of what kinds of employees to look for, business owners can proactively reach out to workers they are interested in, which allows the company to steadily build cohesive and productive teams.

Key Insight 4

Leaders do not allow negative attitudes or team members to derail their efforts.

Analysis

Even if an employee agrees to help a boss accomplish a given project, he or she might still have a negative attitude. That pessimism can spread to the rest of the team and undermine cohesive efforts. Under Joy's sixth rule, team leaders are required to make sure all members of a group know negativity will not be tolerated. If a team member refuses to stop being needlessly critical and pessimistic, a leader may have to fire that employee to prevent the group's efforts from being sabotaged.

In *The Power of a Positive Team: Proven Principles and Practices That Make Great Teams Great* (2018), also by Gordon, he explains that negative team members sometimes don't realize they're being pessimistic, and often don't want to continue behaving in a way that's detrimental to the group effort. Often, leaders just need to meet with negative teammates one by one, so that a genuine conversation can be had about where the pessimism is coming from. The group member might be having a hard time in his or her personal life, or may be suffering from a mental illness like depression. Regardless of the reason behind the negativity, a good leader can listen with empathy, and can provide strategies that will help a group member become a positive addition to the team. Employers should give workers who have been defeatist in the past but who are willing to change a chance to improve their attitudes.

Key Insight 5

Positive attitudes attract new talented workers and motivate existing employees to do their best.

Analysis

Energy and ambition are infectious; employees naturally want to be a part of an effort that spreads happiness among those who are already involved. Joy tells George that the seventh rule demands he remain enthusiastic about his dreams so that he can attract motivated employees and inspire current teammates.

Even if business owners feel enthusiastic about their company, that passion may not be apparent to employees. Lack of outward enthusiasm can make it difficult for that joy to spread to others, which can make an office space emotionally stagnant. A 2013 *Washington Post* column argues that workers and bosses alike can practice several techniques to show enthusiasm on the job. Smiling more and keeping neutral expressions that don't convey boredom or sadness can show employees that a supervisor is committed to staying upbeat about day-to-day tasks. Proactively offering to help workers complete tasks can also convey enthusiasm, and show that a boss is a team player who is not above helping underlings. If workers are willing to perform tasks outside of their designated title, or stay late or come in early at times, then they will be seen as enthusiastic members of the company and will likely be considered for promotions and pay raises. Practicing enthusiasm can even help workers find a new job if they are unhappy at their current workplace. Most employers don't want to hire those who seem to have no energy, but are grateful to meet workers who dedicate themselves fully and passionately to the tasks at hand. By staying enthusiastic, workplace leaders can not only motivate their coworkers, but can also improve their own prospects and get more enjoyment out of work.

Key Insight 6

To retain their trust and loyalty, leaders must show genuine love and concern for their employees.

Analysis

Before George decided he was going to practice positivity, he often neglected to notice the good work of his employees. One of his workers, José, tells George that he turned down the opportunity to help because George never worked to ensure José's promotion, even though José had stayed loyal to his leadership for years. José's anger and frustration helps George learn Joy's eighth rule, which is that employers should connect with their workers and treat them with genuine care.

If employees are stuck with a boss who doesn't care about them, then they likely will be passed over not only for salary raises and promotions, but also for training opportunities and chances to lead new projects. A 2017 *U.S. News & World Report* article explains that employees whose bosses have consistently given them little or no consideration should seek out new jobs immediately, rather than waiting for the current situation to improve. It's possible that once workers have received a better job offer, they can bring the boss's attention to the fact that they are unhappy and ask for a counteroffer. However, a leader who has not shown interest in employees' growth until they threaten to leave will likely remain a lackluster supervisor in the future. A boss who doesn't value employees is additionally likely to underpay them, or pay two workers who perform the same task disparate salaries. Employees should be willing to research what a fair salary is in their trade, and should check with coworkers so that they can have more information about pay inequity in the workplace. If, after meeting with their boss, unhappy employees still cannot get the salaries or recognition they deserve, they should recognize the need to look for a new company with supervisors who do care.

Key Insight 7

Employees and leaders alike must find greater meaning for their work if they wish to stay productive.

Analysis

A new project may energize a team for a while, but if workers don't find a more meaningful reason to complete their tasks, they will quickly lose any momentum sparked by the initial excitement. Even if employees enjoy the profession, they may find it difficult to keep going at a job if they lose sight of the reason for choosing that career in the first place. Joy's ninth rule teaches adherents that they must identify a deeper reason to accomplish goals, and use that motivation to pull through moments when tasks become tedious or boring.

A 2015 *New York Times* opinion piece argues that finding greater meaning in work is the only reason that some professionals choose low-paying jobs over more prestigious careers. Some doctors who could work at high-paying hospitals choose to spend their time caring for patients who are impoverished or living in stagnant communities. Lawyers who could join profitable firms instead choose to work at small community organizations that serve those who have no money to pay for legal representation. These seemingly altruistic workers fly in the face of a common belief that people only seek out jobs to make ends meet and that humans are naturally lazy. Those concepts stem from the writings of Adam Smith, an eighteenth century economist and author who is credited with shaping modern capitalism. Smith believed that most people are disengaged from their jobs, and that all work is income driven. He further believed that as workers' enjoyment of the job went down, their productivity would go up, because they would simply want to complete given tasks faster. However, Smith's concepts have not led to more productivity in the modern workforce, and they overlook employees who remain in low-paying jobs because they believe their role within an organization makes a difference. Job seekers don't simply want a paycheck; they also want engaging work that makes them feel good about themselves. If companies are willing to help employees keep a greater purpose in mind, then they might develop more productive teams and happier office spaces.

Key Insight 8

Leaders must remember to enjoy life, instead of just treating each day as an opportunity to gain money and accolades.

Analysis

Joy's tenth rule instructs her bus riders to seek out happiness in their day-to-day lives. Just because workers are good at a job doesn't mean they are happy. If they are unhappy, and remain so for a long time, it's possible that they won't be able to keep up performance at work, and might become alienated from coworkers and loved ones. Business owners and workers must remember that professional accolades aren't everything, and take time to seek out activities they enjoy.

Employees who are chronically depressed should work on improving their personal lives, but also consider how their environments might be affecting their moods, especially if they are overworked and living in an urban setting. In *The Nature Fix: Why Nature Makes Us Happier, Healthier, and More Creative* (2017), author Florence Williams interviews Finnish researcher Liisa Tyrväinen, who investigates how access to nature improves mental health. Tyrväinen argues that all humans need access to nature, but fewer people have access to it if they live and work in cities. Thankfully, office workers who want to try improving their moods by spending time in nature don't have to worry about rearranging their schedules too much. While humans get the most benefit from spending at least five hours a month in natural settings, study participants who spent anywhere from 15 to 45 minutes in a public park still reported improvements in their moods and overall sense of well being. Employees who have trouble relaxing and getting their minds off work should consider making time for regular walks in their local parks, and should schedule periodic getaways such as camping trips with family members. By staying in touch with nature, a worker can not only become better adjusted, but can begin to enjoy life, both on and off the clock.

Important People

Jon Gordon has authored more than a dozen books on positivity and self-development; *The Energy Bus* was one of his first bestselling works. He also serves as a motivational speaker and consultant.

George is the main character of the allegorical narrative. He is an employee in middle management whose negativity is affecting his job performance and his marriage.

Joy, a cheery bus driver, teaches George 10 laws that will help him use positivity to succeed.

José is a hardworking employee who has become disillusioned because his boss, George, hasn't recognized his efforts.

Author's Style

Jon Gordon could have written a straightforward business book that teaches readers how to use positivity to improve work performance and life satisfaction. Instead, he created a fictional tale in which a burnt-out businessman named George learns how to revitalize his professional and personal life by cultivating a better outlook. Gordon weaves his 10 lessons for creating a positive attitude into his story by making them a primary component of George's journey; each day that George interacts with the bus's optimistic driver, he learns another lesson that moves him closer toward success.

As he has done with previous work, Gordon uses *The Energy Bus* to advertise his services. George at one point is instructed to visit a website and print out tickets for his team inviting them to practice positivity; the same website exists outside the book, and is mentioned again at the conclusion of the story for any interested readers. At the book's end, Gordon provides his contact information for any person or company who might want to hear him speak, and encourages readers to sign up for his newsletter. Gordon's need to insert advertisements can distract from the overall story, and makes clear that each character on the bus, outside of its driver, is meant to serve a perfunctory role.

At less than 200 pages, *The Energy Bus* is a quick read; many of its 34 chapters are barely a page long. The book includes a foreword written by leadership expert Ken Blanchard, as well as a section at the end providing strategies for managers and others who want to build a successful team. An advertisement for Gordon's online training course is additionally included at the end of *The Energy Bus*.

Author's Perspective

Jon Gordon explains in the author's note that a real-life bus driver with an upbeat attitude inspired a popular issue of his newsletter. After his audience told him that his story about the bus driver was helpful, Gordon expanded it into a book. Throughout *The Energy Bus*, Gordon repeatedly asserts that every event in a person's life happens for a reason, and can be used to that person's advantage as long as he or she remains open to the potential message. By recognizing value in the bus driver's positive attitude, Gordon was able to grow as a motivational speaker and capitalize on his affirmative experience.

Gordon reintroduces several of the lessons from *The Energy Bus* in his later books including *The Power of a Positive Team: Proven Principles and Practices That Make Great Teams Great* (2018). Although *The Energy Bus* can be used by individuals who want to improve their attitude, the book can also be applied to teams who are trying to find better camaraderie and cohesion. Gordon especially emphasizes the need to convert, avoid, or overcome those who remain negative in the face of positive thinking. Although Gordon believes that readers must triumph over negativity, he asserts that pessimistic team members should be given multiple opportunities to change. A negative influence on a team can become a positive leader with the right encouragement, just as George became an optimistic force in his workplace.

Printed in Great Britain
by Amazon

10400929R00020